The Mash Cook

50 Delicious Recipes of Mashed Potatoes

BY

Rachael Rayner

Copyright 2020 Rachael Rayner

License Notes

No part of this Book can be reproduced in any form or by any means including print, electronic, scanning or photocopying unless prior permission is granted by the author.

All ideas, suggestions and guidelines mentioned here are written for informative purposes. While the author has taken every possible step to ensure accuracy, all readers are advised to follow information at their own risk. The author cannot be held responsible for personal and/or commercial damages in case of misinterpreting and misunderstanding any part of this Book

Table of Contents

Introduction 7

    Mushroom Potato Mash 9

    Chive Potato Mash 11

    Sweet Potato and Potato Mash 13

    Garlic Potato Mash 15

    Parsley Potato Mash 17

    Onion Potato Mash 19

    Tuna Potato Mash 21

    Tandoori Chicken Potato Mash 23

    Peri Peri Potato Mash 25

    Oregano Potato Mash 27

    Black Peppercorn Potato Mash 29

    Kale Potato Mash 31

    Spinach Potato Mash 33

    Beef Potato Mash 35

Hardboiled Egg Potato Mash	37
Bacon Potato Mash	39
Salami Potato Mash	41
Ham Potato Mash	43
Mint Potato Mash	45
Cumin Potato Mash	47
Cheddar Cheese Potato Mash	49
Carrot Potato Mash	51
Cream Cheese Potato Mash	53
Green Pea and Potato Mash	55
Sour Cream Potato Mash	57
Lentil Potato Mash	59
Rice Potato Mash	61
Cottage Cheese Potato Mash	63
Ginger Potato Mash	65
Coriander Potato Mash	67
Ricotta Potato Mash	69

Jalapeno Potato Mash 71

Paprika Potato Mash 73

Bell Pepper Potato Mash 75

Cauliflower Potato Mash 77

Pumpkin Potato Mash 79

Cabbage Potato Mash 81

Broccoli Potato Mash 83

Curry Potato Mash 85

Greek Yogurt Potato Mash 87

Lemon Potato Mash 89

Avocado Potato Mash 91

Mozzarella Potato Mash 93

Meatball Potato Mash 95

Turkey Potato Mash 97

Salmon Potato Mash 99

Coconut Potato Mash 101

Peanut Potato Mash 103

    Cashew Potato Mash 105

    Tomato Potato Mash 107

Conclusion 109

Author's Afterthoughts 110

Introduction

Mashed potatoes are considered as the most comforting food of America. They are creamy in texture, which everybody loves. But, are you aware of the fact that mashed potatoes can be much more alterable than the classic version?

By including the correct ingredients, mashed potatoes can turn into an ideal side dish or even a main meal for practically any meal, influenced by any culture. From curry mashed potatoes, spinach mashed potatoes, to salami mashed potatoes, and a whole lot many varieties!

In this recipe book, you'll rejuvenate your craving for mashed potatoes with its diverse delicious collection. So put potatoes in a pot and get your potato masher all set and get ready to prepare some delicious mashed potatoes!

The American families love mashed potatoes is a trivialization; it is one of the favourite American foods. The gooey potato tastes best with fresh chopped chives, sour cream or a heap of melted butter or submerged into gravy served with stirred veggies, and steaks can make anyone's mouth-watering and eyes-glowing in hunger.

You will never find food as versatile as a potato that is ideal side dish. Many people like to eat them straight out of the bowl without any main dish, and many also love a chunk of a juicy steak or baked chicken breast with a bite of creamy mash. Smear it with gravy or combine with fried bacon, either way, it is tastes amazing and delightful. The 50 mouth-watering recipes of mashed potato recipes offered in this recipe book will introduce you to a new range of flavours and consistency for any meal.

Mushroom Potato Mash

Mash with stir-fried mushrooms, boiled potatoes, and cream!

Serves: 2

Preparation Time: 15 minutes

Cooking Time: NIL

Ingredients

- Salt and pepper to taste
- 1 cup finely chopped mushrooms, stir-fried
- 4 tablespoons heavy cream
- 2 cups boiled potatoes, mashed

Method

1. Combine all the ingredients in a bowl and mix well.

2. Serve warm!

Chive Potato Mash

Mash with chives, boiled potatoes, and cream!

Serves: 2

Preparation Time: 15 minutes

Cooking Time: NIL

Ingredients

- 3 cups boiled potatoes, mashed
- 4 tablespoons chives, finely chopped
- 4 tablespoons heavy cream
- Salt and pepper to taste

Method

1. Combine all the ingredients in a bowl and mix well.

2. Serve warm!

Sweet Potato and Potato Mash

Mash with sweet potatoes, boiled potatoes, and cream!

Serves: 2

Preparation Time: 15 minutes

Cooking Time: NIL

Ingredients

- Salt and pepper to taste
- 1 cup boiled sweet potatoes, chopped
- 4 tablespoons heavy cream
- 2 cups boiled potatoes, mashed

Method

1. Combine all the ingredients in a bowl and mix well.

2. Serve warm!

Garlic Potato Mash

Mash with stir-fried garlic boiled potatoes, and cream!

Serves: 2

Preparation Time: 15 minutes

Cooking Time: NIL

Ingredients

- 3 cups boiled potatoes, mashed
- 2 tablespoons finely chopped garlic, stir fried
- 4 tablespoons heavy cream
- Salt and pepper to taste

Method

1. Combine all the ingredients in a bowl and mix well.

2. Serve warm!

Parsley Potato Mash

Mash with fresh parsley leaves, boiled potatoes, and cream!

Serves: 2

Preparation Time: 15 minutes

Cooking Time: NIL

Ingredients

- Salt and pepper to taste
- 1 cup fresh parsley leaves, finely chopped
- 4 tablespoons heavy cream
- 2 cups boiled potatoes, mashed

Method

1. Combine all the ingredients in a bowl and mix well.

2. Serve warm!

Onion Potato Mash

Mash with stir-fried mushrooms, boiled potatoes, and cream!

Serves: 2

Preparation Time: 15 minutes

Cooking Time: NIL

Ingredients

- 2 cups boiled potatoes, mashed
- 1 cup finally chopped onion, stir-fried until translucent
- 4 tablespoons heavy cream
- Salt and pepper to taste

Method

1. Combine all the ingredients in a bowl and mix well.

2. Serve warm!

Tuna Potato Mash

Mash with tuna flakes, boiled potatoes, and cream!

Serves: 2

Preparation Time: 15 minutes

Cooking Time: NIL

Ingredients

- 2 cups boiled potatoes, mashed
- 1 cup canned tuna flakes
- 4 tablespoons heavy cream
- Salt and pepper to taste

Method

1. Combine all the ingredients in a bowl and mix well.

2. Serve warm!

Tandoori Chicken Potato Mash

Mash with shredded tandoori chicken, boiled potatoes, and cream!

Serves: 2

Preparation Time: 15 minutes

Cooking Time: NIL

Ingredients

- Salt and pepper to taste
- 1 cup tandoori chicken, shredded
- 4 tablespoons heavy cream
- 2 cups boiled potatoes, mashed

Method

1. Combine all the ingredients in a bowl and mix well.

2. Serve warm!

Peri Peri Potato Mash

Mash with peri peri seasoning, boiled potatoes, and cream!

Serves: 2

Preparation Time: 15 minutes

Cooking Time: NIL

Ingredients

- 3 cups boiled potatoes, mashed
- 2 teaspoons peri peri seasoning
- Salt to taste
- 4 tablespoons heavy cream

Method

1. Combine all the ingredients in a bowl and mix well.

2. Serve warm!

Oregano Potato Mash

Mash with dry oregano seasoning, boiled potatoes, and cream!

Serves: 2

Preparation Time: 15 minutes

Cooking Time: NIL

Ingredients

- 3 cups boiled potatoes, mashed
- Salt and pepper to taste
- 2 teaspoons dry oregano seasoning
- 4 tablespoons heavy cream

Method

1. Combine all the ingredients in a bowl and mix well.

2. Serve warm!

Black Peppercorn Potato Mash

Mash with black peppercorn, boiled potatoes, and cream!

Serves: 2

Preparation Time: 15 minutes

Cooking Time: NIL

Ingredients

- 3 cups boiled potatoes, mashed
- Salt to taste
- 2 teaspoons freshly crushed black peppercorn
- 4 tablespoons heavy cream

Method

1. Combine all the ingredients in a bowl and mix well.

2. Serve warm!

Kale Potato Mash

Mash with kale leaves, boiled potatoes, and cream!

Serves: 2

Preparation Time: 15 minutes

Cooking Time: NIL

Ingredients

- 2 cups boiled potatoes, mashed
- 1 cup kale leaves, finely chopped
- 4 tablespoons heavy cream
- Salt and pepper to taste

Method

1. Combine all the ingredients in a bowl and mix well.

2. Serve warm!

Spinach Potato Mash

Mash with baby spinach leaves, boiled potatoes, and cream!

Serves: 2

Preparation Time: 15 minutes

Cooking Time: NIL

Ingredients

- 2 cups boiled potatoes, mashed
- 1 cup spinach leaves, finely chopped
- 4 tablespoons heavy cream
- Salt and pepper to taste

Method

1. Combine all the ingredients in a bowl and mix well.

2. Serve warm!

Beef Potato Mash

Mash with stir-fried minced beef, boiled potatoes, and cream!

Serves: 2

Preparation Time: 15 minutes

Cooking Time: NIL

Ingredients

- 2 cups boiled potatoes, mashed
- Salt and pepper to taste
- 1 cup stir-fried minced beef
- 4 tablespoons heavy cream

Method

1. Combine all the ingredients in a bowl and mix well.

2. Serve warm!

Hardboiled Egg Potato Mash

Mash with hard-boiled eggs, boiled potatoes, and cream!

Serves: 2

Preparation Time: 15 minutes

Cooking Time: NIL

Ingredients

- 2 cups boiled potatoes, mashed
- 4 hardboiled eggs, peeled and finely chopped
- 4 tablespoons heavy cream
- Salt and pepper to taste

Method

1. Combine all the ingredients in a bowl and mix well.

2. Serve warm!

Bacon Potato Mash

Mash with crispy bacon, boiled potatoes, and cream!

Serves: 2

Preparation Time: 15 minutes

Cooking Time: NIL

Ingredients

- 2 cups boiled potatoes, mashed
- 1 cup fried bacon, crushed
- 4 tablespoons heavy cream
- Salt and pepper to taste

Method

1. Combine all the ingredients in a bowl and mix well.

2. Serve warm!

Salami Potato Mash

Mash with salami, boiled potatoes, and cream!

Serves: 2

Preparation Time: 15 minutes

Cooking Time: NIL

Ingredients

- 2 cups boiled potatoes, mashed
- Salt and pepper to taste
- 1 cup salami, finely chopped
- 4 tablespoons heavy cream

Method

1. Combine all the ingredients in a bowl and mix well.

2. Serve warm!

Ham Potato Mash

Mash with ham, boiled potatoes, and cream!

Serves: 2

Preparation Time: 15 minutes

Cooking Time: NIL

Ingredients

- 2 cups boiled potatoes, mashed
- 1 cup ham, finely chopped
- Salt and pepper to taste
- 4 tablespoons heavy cream

Method

1. Combine all the ingredients in a bowl and mix well.

2. Serve warm!

Mint Potato Mash

Mash with fresh mint leaves, boiled potatoes, and cream!

Serves: 2

Preparation Time: 15 minutes

Cooking Time: NIL

Ingredients

- 2 cups boiled potatoes, mashed
- Salt and pepper to taste
- 1 cup mint leaves, finely chopped
- 4 tablespoons heavy cream

Method

1. Combine all the ingredients in a bowl and mix well.

2. Serve warm!

Cumin Potato Mash

Mash with roasted cumin, boiled potatoes, and cream!

Serves: 2

Preparation Time: 15 minutes

Cooking Time: NIL

Ingredients

- 3 cups boiled potatoes, mashed
- 2 teaspoons roasted cumin powder
- 4 tablespoons heavy cream
- Salt and pepper to taste

Method

1. Combine all the ingredients in a bowl and mix well.

2. Serve warm!

Cheddar Cheese Potato Mash

Mash with cheddar cheese, boiled potatoes, and cream!

Serves: 2

Preparation Time: 15 minutes

Cooking Time: NIL

Ingredients

- Salt and pepper to taste
- 2 cups boiled potatoes, mashed
- 1 cup cheddar cheese, grated
- 4 tablespoons heavy cream

Method

1. Combine all the ingredients in a bowl and mix well.

2. Serve warm!

Carrot Potato Mash

Mash with carrot, boiled potatoes, and cream!

Serves: 2

Preparation Time: 15 minutes

Cooking Time: NIL

Ingredients

- 2 cups boiled potatoes, mashed
- 1 cup boiled carrots, mashed
- 4 tablespoons heavy cream
- Salt and pepper to taste

Method

1. Combine all the ingredients in a bowl and mix well.

2. Serve warm!

Cream Cheese Potato Mash

Mash with cream cheese, boiled potatoes, and cream!

Serves: 2

Preparation Time: 15 minutes

Cooking Time: NIL

Ingredients

- 2 cups boiled potatoes, mashed
- 1 cup cream cheese
- Salt and pepper to taste
- 4 tablespoons heavy cream

Method

1. Combine all the ingredients in a bowl and mix well.

2. Serve warm!

Green Pea and Potato Mash

Mash with green peas, boiled potatoes, and cream!

Serves: 2

Preparation Time: 15 minutes

Cooking Time: NIL

Ingredients

- 2 cups boiled potatoes, mashed
- 1 cup mashed green peas
- Salt and pepper to taste
- 4 tablespoons heavy cream

Method

1. Combine all the ingredients in a bowl and mix well.

2. Serve warm!

Sour Cream Potato Mash

Mash with boiled potatoes and sour cream!

Serves: 2

Preparation Time: 15 minutes

Cooking Time: NIL

Ingredients

- Salt and pepper to taste
- 3 cups boiled potatoes, mashed
- 1/2 cup sour cream

Method

1. Combine all the ingredients in a bowl and mix well.

2. Serve warm!

Lentil Potato Mash

Mash with lentils, boiled potatoes, and cream!

Serves: 2

Preparation Time: 15 minutes

Cooking Time: NIL

Ingredients

- 2 cups boiled potatoes, mashed
- 1 cup boiled and mashed lentils
- 4 tablespoons heavy cream
- Salt and pepper to taste

Method

1. Combine all the ingredients in a bowl and mix well.

2. Serve warm!

Rice Potato Mash

Mash with rice, boiled potatoes, and cream!

Serves: 2

Preparation Time: 15 minutes

Cooking Time: NIL

Ingredients

- Salt and pepper to taste
- 1 cup boiled and mashed white rice
- 4 tablespoons heavy cream
- 2 cups boiled potatoes, mashed

Method

1. Combine all the ingredients in a bowl and mix well.

2. Serve warm!

Cottage Cheese Potato Mash

Mash with cottage cheese, boiled potatoes, and cream!

Serves: 2

Preparation Time: 15 minutes

Cooking Time: NIL

Ingredients

- Salt and pepper to taste
- 2 cups boiled potatoes, mashed
- 1 cup crumbled cottage cheese
- 4 tablespoons heavy cream

Method

1. Combine all the ingredients in a bowl and mix well.

2. Serve warm!

Ginger Potato Mash

Mash with ginger, boiled potatoes, and cream!

Serves: 2

Preparation Time: 15 minutes

Cooking Time: NIL

Ingredients

- Salt and pepper to taste
- 3 cups boiled potatoes, mashed
- 2 teaspoons ginger, grated
- 4 tablespoons heavy cream

Method

1. Combine all the ingredients in a bowl and mix well.

2. Serve warm!

Coriander Potato Mash

Mash with coriander leaves, boiled potatoes, and cream!

Serves: 2

Preparation Time: 15 minutes

Cooking Time: NIL

Ingredients

- 2 cups boiled potatoes, mashed
- 1 cup coriander leaves, finely chopped
- 4 tablespoons heavy cream
- Salt and pepper to taste

Method

1. Combine all the ingredients in a bowl and mix well.

2. Serve warm!

Ricotta Potato Mash

Mash with ricotta cheese, boiled potatoes, and cream!

Serves: 2

Preparation Time: 15 minutes

Cooking Time: NIL

Ingredients

- Salt and pepper to taste
- 2 cups boiled potatoes, mashed
- 1 cup ricotta cheese, crumbled
- 4 tablespoons heavy cream

Method

1. Combine all the ingredients in a bowl and mix well.

2. Serve warm!

Jalapeno Potato Mash

Mash with pickled jalapeños, boiled potatoes, and cream!

Serves: 2

Preparation Time: 15 minutes

Cooking Time: NIL

Ingredients

- 3 cups boiled potatoes, mashed
- 1/2 cup pickled jalapeños, finely chopped
- 4 tablespoons heavy cream
- Salt and pepper to taste

Method

1. Combine all the ingredients in a bowl and mix well.

2. Serve warm!

Paprika Potato Mash

Mash with stir-fried mushrooms, boiled potatoes, and cream!

Serves: 2

Preparation Time: 15 minutes

Cooking Time: NIL

Ingredients

- Salt and pepper to taste
- 3 cups boiled potatoes, mashed
- 1 teaspoon, paprika
- 4 tablespoons heavy cream

Method

1. Combine all the ingredients in a bowl and mix well.

2. Serve warm!

Bell Pepper Potato Mash

Mash with green bell pepper, boiled potatoes, and cream!

Serves: 2

Preparation Time: 15 minutes

Cooking Time: NIL

Ingredients

- 2 cups boiled potatoes, mashed
- 1 cup green bell pepper, finely chopped
- 4 tablespoons heavy cream
- Salt and pepper to taste

Method

1. Combine all the ingredients in a bowl and mix well.

2. Serve warm!

Cauliflower Potato Mash

Mash with cauliflower, boiled potatoes, and cream!

Serves: 2

Preparation Time: 15 minutes

Cooking Time: NIL

Ingredients

- Salt and pepper to taste
- 2 cups boiled potatoes, mashed
- 1 cup boiled and mashed, cauliflower florets
- 4 tablespoons heavy cream

Method

1. Combine all the ingredients in a bowl and mix well.

2. Serve warm!

Pumpkin Potato Mash

Mash with pumpkin, boiled potatoes, and cream!

Serves: 2

Preparation Time: 15 minutes

Cooking Time: NIL

Ingredients

- 2 cups boiled potatoes, mashed
- 1 cup boiled and mashed pumpkin
- 4 tablespoons heavy cream
- Salt and pepper to taste

Method

1. Combine all the ingredients in a bowl and mix well.

2. Serve warm!

Cabbage Potato Mash

Mash with cabbage, boiled potatoes, and cream!

Serves: 2

Preparation Time: 15 minutes

Cooking Time: NIL

Ingredients

- 2 cups boiled potatoes, mashed
- 1 cup boiled and mashed cabbage
- 4 tablespoons heavy cream
- Salt and pepper to taste

Method

1. Combine all the ingredients in a bowl and mix well.

2. Serve warm!

Broccoli Potato Mash

Mash with broccoli, boiled potatoes, and cream!

Serves: 2

Preparation Time: 15 minutes

Cooking Time: NIL

Ingredients

- 2 cups boiled potatoes, mashed
- 1 cup boiled and mashed broccoli
- 4 tablespoons heavy cream
- Salt and pepper to taste

Method

1. Combine all the ingredients in a bowl and mix well.

2. Serve warm!

Curry Potato Mash

Mash with curry powder, boiled potatoes, and cream!

Serves: 2

Preparation Time: 15 minutes

Cooking Time: NIL

Ingredients

- Salt to taste
- 3 cups boiled potatoes, mashed
- 1 teaspoon curry powder
- 4 tablespoons heavy cream

Method

1. Combine all the ingredients in a bowl and mix well.

2. Serve warm!

Greek Yogurt Potato Mash

Mash with Greek yogurt and boiled potatoes!

Serves: 2

Preparation Time: 15 minutes

Cooking Time: NIL

Ingredients

- Salt and pepper to taste
- 3 cups boiled potatoes, mashed
- 1/2 cup Greek yogurt

Method

1. Combine all the ingredients in a bowl and mix well.

2. Serve warm!

Lemon Potato Mash

Mash with boiled potatoes and lemon!

Serves: 2

Preparation Time: 15 minutes

Cooking Time: NIL

Ingredients

- Salt and pepper to taste
- 3 cups boiled potatoes, mashed
- Juice of 1 lemon

Method

1. Combine all the ingredients in a bowl and mix well.

2. Serve warm!

Avocado Potato Mash

Mash with avocado, boiled potatoes, and cream!

Serves: 2

Preparation Time: 15 minutes

Cooking Time: NIL

Ingredients

- 2 cups boiled potatoes, mashed
- 1 cup avocado pulp, mashed
- 4 tablespoons heavy cream
- Salt and pepper to taste

Method

1. Combine all the ingredients in a bowl and mix well.

2. Serve warm!

Mozzarella Potato Mash

Mash with mozzarella cheese, boiled potatoes, and cream!

Serves: 2

Preparation Time: 15 minutes

Cooking Time: NIL

Ingredients

- Salt and pepper to taste
- 2 cups boiled potatoes, mashed
- 1 cup mozzarella cheese, grated
- 4 tablespoons heavy cream

Method

1. Combine all the ingredients in a bowl and mix well.

2. Serve warm!

Meatball Potato Mash

Mash with mashed meatballs, boiled potatoes, and cream!

Serves: 2

Preparation Time: 15 minutes

Cooking Time: NIL

Ingredients

- Salt and pepper to taste
- 2 cups boiled potatoes, mashed
- 1 cup mashed meatballs
- 4 tablespoons heavy cream

Method

1. Combine all the ingredients in a bowl and mix well.

2. Serve warm!

Turkey Potato Mash

Mash with roasted turkey, boiled potatoes, and cream!

Serves: 2

Preparation Time: 15 minutes

Cooking Time: NIL

Ingredients

- Salt and pepper to taste
- 2 cups boiled potatoes, mashed
- 1 cup roasted turkey, shredded
- 4 tablespoons heavy cream

Method

1. Combine all the ingredients in a bowl and mix well.

2. Serve warm!

Salmon Potato Mash

Mash with salmon, boiled potatoes, and cream!

Serves: 2

Preparation Time: 15 minutes

Cooking Time: NIL

Ingredients

- 2 cups boiled potatoes, mashed
- 1 cup cooked salmon, flaked
- 4 tablespoons heavy cream
- Salt and pepper to taste

Method

1. Combine all the ingredients in a bowl and mix well.

2. Serve warm!

Coconut Potato Mash

Mash with boiled potatoes and coconut cream!

Serves: 2

Preparation Time: 15 minutes

Cooking Time: NIL

Ingredients

- Salt and pepper to taste
- 3 cups boiled potatoes, mashed
- 1/4 cup coconut cream

Method

1. Combine all the ingredients in a bowl and mix well.

2. Serve warm!

Peanut Potato Mash

Mash with roasted peanuts, boiled potatoes, and cream!

Serves: 2

Preparation Time: 15 minutes

Cooking Time: NIL

Ingredients

- Salt and pepper to taste
- 2 cups boiled potatoes, mashed
- 1 cup roasted peanuts, crushed
- 4 tablespoons heavy cream

Method

1. Combine all the ingredients in a bowl and mix well.

2. Serve warm!

Cashew Potato Mash

Mash with cashew puree, boiled potatoes, and cream!

Serves: 2

Preparation Time: 15 minutes

Cooking Time: NIL

Ingredients

- Salt and pepper to taste
- 2 1/2 cups boiled potatoes, mashed
- 1/2 cup cashew, pureed
- 4 tablespoons heavy cream

Method

1. Combine all the ingredients in a bowl and mix well.

2. Serve warm!

Tomato Potato Mash

Mash with stir fried mushrooms, boiled potatoes, and cream!

Serves: 2

Preparation Time: 15 minutes

Cooking Time: NIL

Ingredients

- Salt and pepper to taste
- 2 1/2 cups boiled potatoes, mashed
- 1/2 cup tomato puree
- 4 tablespoons heavy cream

Method

1. Combine all the ingredients in a bowl and mix well.

2. Serve warm!

Conclusion

This cookbook offers the best and very unique recipes of mashed potatoes.

Come and take this delicious journey with us into the world of delights of quick cooking. The motto of this recipe book is to epitomize the effortless nature of easy cooking.

In this recipe book, we have focused on mashed potatoes. The Mashed Cookbook is a comprehensive set of easy but very innovative mashed potato recipes. You will realize after reading this cookbook that even though all the recipes are super simple, they all taste quite delicious.

Enjoy!

Author's Afterthoughts

Thanks ever so much to each of my cherished readers for investing the time to read this book!

I know you could have picked from many other books, but you chose this one. So, a big thanks for downloading this book and reading all the way to the end.

If you enjoyed this book or received value from it, I'd like to ask you for a favor. Please take a few minutes to post an honest and heartfelt review on Amazon.com. Your support does make a difference and helps to benefit other people.

Thanks for your Reviews!

Rachael Rayner

Printed in Great Britain
by Amazon